About the Author™

Meet
Beverly Cleary

S. Ward

The Rosen Publishing Group's
PowerKids Press™
New York

Published in 2001 by The Rosen Publishing Group, Inc.
29 East 21st Street, New York, NY 10010

First Edition

Book Design: Maria Melendez

Photo Credits: Cover, title page, p. 4 © The Everett Collection; p. 7 © Bettmann/CORBIS; p. 8, 11, 12, 19 © Archive Photos; p. 9, 13 © Underwood & Underwood/CORBIS; p. 14 © CORBIS; p. 20 by Thaddeus Harden.

Grateful acknowledgment is made for permission to reprint previously published material on pp. 15, 16, 18, 20, 21, and 22: from RAMONA THE PEST by Beverly Cleary, illustrated by Louis Darling, copyright 1968 by Beverly Cleary; BEEZUS AND RAMONA by Beverly Cleary, illustrated by Louis Darling, copyright 1955 by Beverly Cleary; RAMONA AND HER FATHER by Beverly Cleary, copyright 1975, 1977 by Beverly Cleary, illustrated by Alan Tiegreen; and RAMONA QUIMBY, AGE 8 by Beverly Cleary, copyright 1981 by Beverly Cleary, illustrated by Alan Tiegreen, published by arrangement with William Morrow and Company, Inc., and used with permission by Avon Books, Inc.

Ward, S. (Stasia), 1968–
   Meet Beverly Cleary / S. Ward.—1st ed.
     p. cm.— (About the author)
   Includes index.
   Summary: A simple biography of the prolific children's author, Beverly Cleary, whose prize-winning writing career spans fifty years.
   ISBN 0-8239-5710-1 (alk. paper)
   1. Cleary, Beverly—Juvenile literature. 2. Authors, American—20th century—Biography—Juvenile literature. 3. Women librarians—United States—Biography—Juvenile literature. 4. Librarians—United States—Biography—Juvenile literature. 5. Children's stories—Authorship—Juvenile literature. [1. Cleary, Beverly. 2. Authors, American. 3. Women—Biography.] I. Title. II. Series.

PS3553.L3914 Z9 2001
813'.54—dc21
[B]
                                                             00-024211

Contents

beverly cleary

Henry Huggins

In 1950, Beverly Cleary sent a story to the William Morrow publishing company. Beverly's story was called "Spareribs and Henry." The story is about a boy named Henry. Henry finds a stray dog. He names the dog Ribsy. Henry and Ribsy have lots of fun **adventures**. The children's book **editor** at William Morrow loved Beverly's writing. She accepted "Spareribs and Henry" to be **published** as a book.

When the book was published it was given a new title. It was called *Henry Huggins*. Beverly was on her way to becoming one of America's best-loved children's book writers.

Beverly Cleary's editor at William Morrow publishing company was named Elisabeth Hamilton. In just six weeks Elisabeth accepted Beverly's story to be published as a book. In September 1950, Henry Huggins was published. Beverly wrote five more books about Henry and his dog, Ribsy.

◀ *Beverly Cleary is shown here sitting on a statue of Ribsy in the Beverly Cleary Sculpture Garden in Portland, Oregon.*

Farm Child

Going to a neighbor's house to look at a colorful picture book is one of Beverly's favorite childhood memories.

Beverly Atlee Bunn was born on April 12, 1916, in McMinnville, Oregon. She was the only child of Chester and Mable Bunn. Her family lived on a farm in the little town of Yamhill.

Beverly loved living on the farm. She also loved books. She owned only two of them. The books were *Mother Goose* and *The Three Bears*.

Yamhill did not have a public library until Beverly was five years old. At that time her mother helped start the town's first library. Beverly was thrilled to find many more stories to read.

This picture of a farm in Oregon was taken around the time Beverly was a little girl. She and her family lived on a farm in Yamhill, Oregon. ▶

City Girl

When Beverly was six years old, her family moved to Portland, Oregon. Portland was a big city. It was very different from Yamhill. Beverly liked her new neighborhood. There were lots of other children. She liked the big children's room at the Portland Library.

Beverly did not like going to school. She wanted to be on the farm. She did not like her **strict** first grade teacher. She did not even like learning to read. Her teacher divided readers into three groups. Bluebirds were the best readers. Redbirds were the next best readers. Blackbirds were the worst. Beverly was unhappy to be a blackbird.

A city street in Portland, Oregon.

◀ The city of Portland is the largest city in Oregon. Beverly was six years old when she and her family moved there.

Making Plans

Beverly liked her second grade teacher. She began to enjoy reading. Her writing got better, too. When Beverly was in the seventh grade, her library teacher told her that she should write for children when she grew up. Beverly thought this was a good idea. She also wanted to be a **librarian**. She would need to go to college to get this kind of job. College cost money, though. Her family did not have a lot of money. Then her father lost his job. It was hard to find another job because this was during the time of the **Great Depression**.

The Great Depression was a money crisis that began in 1929 and lasted until about 1939. Many Americans, like the ones pictured here, lost their jobs.

College and Marriage

Beverly's cousin, Verna, invited Beverly to come live with her in California. There, she could attend **junior college** for free. She studied English at a junior college. Then she attended the University of California at Berkeley and earned her **degree**. In 1939, she also earned a degree from the School of Librarianship at the University of Washington. Beverly's first job out of school was as a children's librarian in Yakima, Washington.

While at college, Beverly had met Clarence T. Cleary. Beverly and Clarence got married in 1940. They lived in California.

Beverly earned a degree from the University of Washington.

Beverly met Clarence T. Cleary at the University of California, Berkeley. After she and Clarence were married, they lived in Oakland, California, and then moved to Berkeley.

Time to Write

While in Oakland, Beverly had been very busy as a librarian. She did not work as a librarian when she moved to Berkeley. She told Clarence she wanted to write a book. He asked her why she was not writing. She joked that they never had any sharp pencils. The next day, Clarence brought home a pencil sharpener. She realized that it was time to begin writing her first book.

Beverly started her first book on January 2, 1950. Each chapter told about one of the adventures of Henry Huggins and his dog, Ribsy. She finished writing the book in just two months.

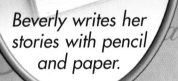

Beverly writes her stories with pencil and paper.

This illustration of Henry, Ribsy, and Ramona is printed in Ramona the Pest. Beverly's book was illustrated by the artist Louis Darling. ▶

Klickitat Street and Beyond

Henry Huggins lived on Klickitat Street. Klickitat Street is a real street in Portland, Oregon. Beverly had lived near there while she was growing up. Beverly made up a group of **imaginary** children who lived on Klickitat Street for her books. These children included Henry, Scooter, Beezus, and Ramona. Beverly has written more than a dozen books that take place around Klickitat Street.

She also wrote stories about other places. A brave mouse named Ralph lived at the Mountain View Inn in *The Mouse and the Motorcycle*, *Ralph S. Mouse*, and *Runaway Ralph*.

Beverly also wrote stories about places besides Klickitat Street. Emily's Runaway Imagination takes place on a farm like the one where Beverly was born. Dear Mr. Henshaw is about a thoughtful young writer named Leigh Botts who lives in a poor California town.

9577

◀ *In this picture, Ramona pedals her tricycle into the coffee table while Beezus and Henry are playing a game of checkers.*

"In the middle of the night Ramona found herself suddenly awake without knowing why she was awake. Had she heard a noise? Yes, she had. Tense, she listened hard. There it was again, a sort of thumping, scuffling noise, not very loud but there just the same. . . ."

—from p. 74 of
Ramona and Her Father

Ideas About Writing

When Beverly was a child, she did not like stories about **magical** fairies or lost princesses. As a grown-up, she writes stories about **ordinary** children who figure out how to solve their problems by themselves. Some of her ideas for her stories come from memories of her childhood. They also come from memories of raising her twin children, Marianne Elisabeth and Malcolm James. Other ideas for stories come from her **imagination**. She does not ask others for ideas while she is writing. She believes that trying to take advice from many different people is not always good for a story.

Beverly based some of the characters in her books on children she played with as a little girl. ▶

Prizes for Beverly

Since she wrote her first book in 1950, Beverly has not stopped writing. She has written over 20 books for children. Beverly's books have won lots of prizes. Young readers, parents, book critics, and librarians have chosen Beverly's books as some of the best they have ever read. In 1983, Beverly wrote a book called *Dear Mr. Henshaw*. The story is about a young boy who writes letters to his favorite author. The story won an important award. The award is called the Newbery Medal. The Newbery Medal is given to the children's book that is voted the best of the year.

"Ramona did not want her fingernails painted by Willa Jean and knew she would be blamed if Willa Jean spilled nail polish."

—from p. 170 of Ramona Quimby, Age 8

Beverly's book Ramona Quimby, Age 8 was named a Newbery Honor Book. Beverly has won many prizes for her books, including awards based on readers' favorites.

Ramona's World

In 1999, a new book was published. This book is called *Ramona's World*. It is a new story about Ramona Quimby of Klickitat Street. In this story, Ramona starts the fourth grade. She has a new teacher, a new best friend, and a new baby sister. Ramona is growing up. Many of Beverly's fans are now grown-ups. Beverly has been writing for 50 years. Some grown-ups read her stories when they were children. Now they are sharing her stories with their own children. Beverly has proven that stories about ordinary children and everyday things make very special books.

An illustration from p. 63 of Ramona Quimby, Age 8.

Glossary

adventures (ad-VEN-cherz) Unusual or exciting things to do.

degree (duh-GREE) A title given by a college to a student who graduates.

editor (EH-dih-ter) The person in charge of correcting errors, checking facts, and deciding what will be printed in a newspaper, book, or magazine.

Great Depression (GRAYT de-PREH-shun) A time in the 1930s when banks and businesses lost money, causing many people to lose their jobs.

imaginary (ih-MA-jih-nayr-ee) Something that is not real or is made up.

imagination (ih-ma-jih-NAY-shun) The ability to create things in your mind.

junior college (JOON-yer KAHL-ej) A school that a student sometimes attends after high school. It usually lasts two years.

librarian (ly-BRAR-ee-un) A person in charge of a collection of books at a library.

magical (MAH-jih-kul) Something or someone that is made up and has strange or special powers.

ordinary (or-DIN-ayr-ee) Common, regular, or everyday.

published (PUH-blishd) Something that is printed for people to read.

strict (STRIKT) Very careful in following a rule or making others follow it.

Index

Web Sites

To learn more about Beverly Cleary, check out these Web sites:

http://www.multnomah.lib.or.us/lib/homework/lithc.html

http://www.teleport.com/~krp/cleary.html

Date Due

BRODART, INC.   Cat. No. 23 233   Printed in U.